# Daffodil Spring

by Irena Freeman
illustrated by Graham Smith

## Harcourt
SCHOOL PUBLISHERS

Printed in the United States of America

ISBN 10: 0-15-350490-0
ISBN 13: 978-0-15-350490-7

Ordering Options
ISBN 10: 0-15-350333-5 (Grade 3 Below-Level Collection)
ISBN 13: 978-0-15-350333-7 (Grade 3 Below-Level Collection)
ISBN 10: 0-15-357476-3 (package of 5)
ISBN 13: 978-0-15-357476-4 (package of 5)

1 2 3 4 5 6 7 8 9 10 179 12 11 10 09 08 07 06

Flowers tell us that it is spring. One of the first flowers of spring is the daffodil. The daffodil brings color back to the world. It lets us know that nice days will come soon.

Daffodils often grow together. They nod in the rustling wind.

How do daffodils grow? People think
that plants grow from seeds. Daffodils can
grow from seeds, but they usually grow
another way. They grow from bulbs.

Daffodil bulbs keep the plants alive a
long time. They also make new daffodils
in a special way.

Many plants live only one season. Daffodils can live for years. They grow in spring. They make their flowers. Then the flowers fall off. The bulbs rest underground and wait for the next season. They stay alive throughout the year. They store food for the plants that will bloom again next spring.

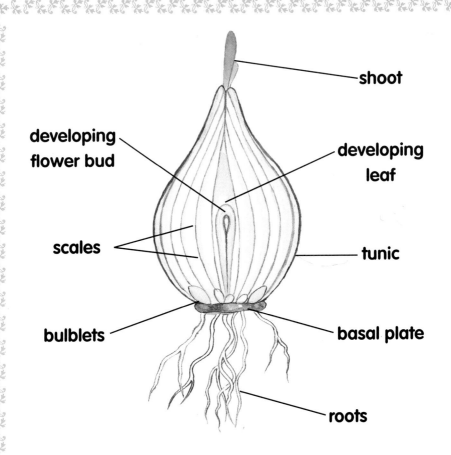

shoot

developing
flower bud

developing
leaf

scales

tunic

bulblets

basal plate

roots

   A daffodil bulb looks like an onion.
There are many parts to a bulb. Each part
many does something different.
   On the outside edge of the bulb is a
tough skin called a tunic. This skin protects
the rest of the bulb. Inside the bulb are soft
scales that store food for the plant.

The bulb waits for spring in the cold ground. If a bulb doesn't stay cold enough in winter, the daffodil will not grow well.

The bulb begins to awaken. From inside the bulb, a small green shoot pushes upward. Roots grow down from a flat place at the bottom of the bulb.

The shoot peeps out from under the ground. The shoot will become leaves. The leaves will gather sun. Far down in the shoot is the bud. It will become the stem and flower.

The roots grow strongly now. They absorb water and food for the plant.

Columns of green shoots surge from the ground. They grow longer and longer. The first shoots become leaves.

Next, the stem begins to grow. It grows from the center of the shoot.

As the stem gets longer, a yellow bud appears at its tip. The bud begins to get bigger. More and more yellow appears.

At last, the flower blooms. The flower may last for a few weeks. Then it falls from the plant. The petals dissolve on the ground.

Daffodils do make seeds. Wind or insects may bring pollen from another daffodil. Then seeds grow in a pod just behind the flower. When the flower falls, the pod will release the seeds. They may grow into other daffodils, but they will take years to bloom.

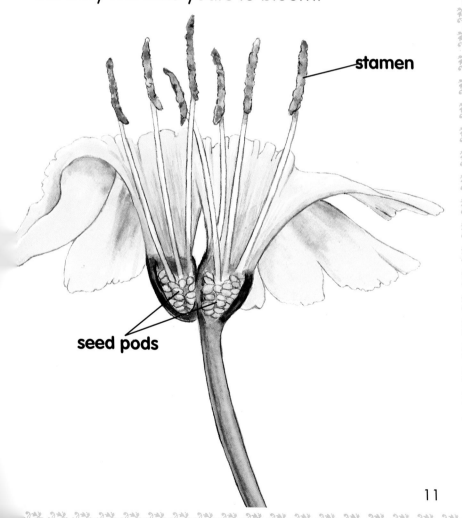

stamen

seed pods

There is another way daffodils grow. The secret is in the bulb. Near the base of the bulb are small particles called *bulblets*. After the flower falls, the plant sends energy to the bulb. The bulblets grow larger. They become bulbs themselves. They are still joined to the first bulb.

Next year, the new bulbs will send up shoots, too. These plants are just like the ones from the first bulb. Most daffodils grow in this way. They spread out in patches.

In early summer, daffodil bulbs rest. The flowers have fallen. The leaves have dried up. Gardeners can dig up the bulbs then. They can be divided and moved to new places. More daffodils will grow. In the spring, they will bring a sunny end to a long winter.

# Think Critically

**1.** What was the purpose of this book?

**2.** How does a daffodil let us know "that nice days will come soon"?

**3.** What is the difference between a daffodil stem and a leaf?

**4.** What is a bulblet and what does it do?

**5.** If you could ask this author a question, what would it be?

 **Science**

**Make a Diagram** Make a diagram with drawings to show the steps of a daffodil's growth during a year. Your diagram should show at least five steps: bulb, root, leaf, bud, and flower.

**School-Home Connection** Most people have a favorite flower. Ask friends and family members what their favorite flowers are. Keep a count of what they say to see which flower people like the most.

**Word Count:** 551